KT-571-692

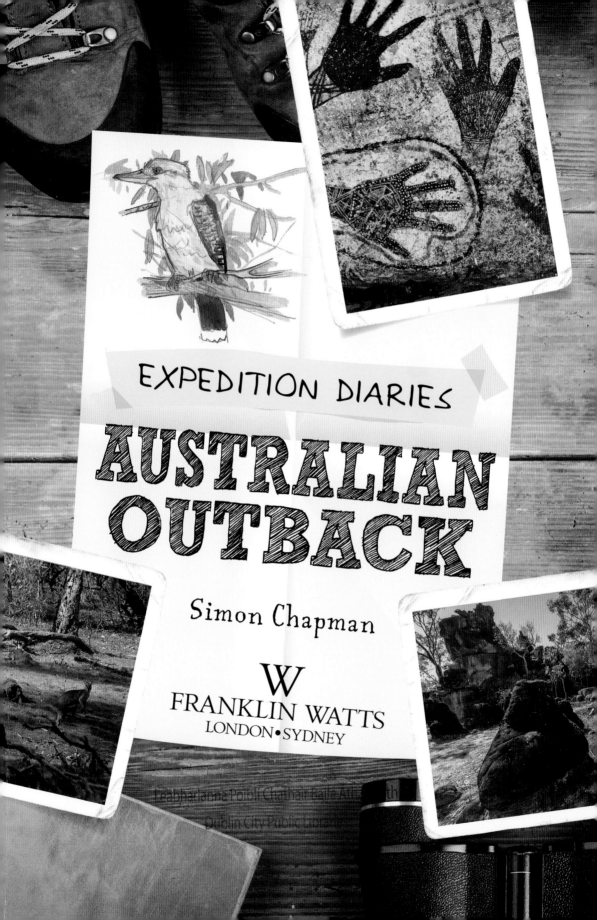

EXPEDITION DIARIES

AUSTRALIAN OUTBACK

Simon Chapman

W
FRANKLIN WATTS
LONDON · SYDNEY

Expedition to the Northern Territory

The plan is to hire a four-wheel drive to tour around Kakadu National Park in Australia's Northern Territory. Kakadu is a famous wilderness of tumbled red rocks and wild wetlands, home to ancient rock paintings, countless kangaroos and the biggest crocodiles in the world!

Personal kit list
- Clothing: lightweight, light-coloured shirt, zip-off trousers that convert into shorts
- Sunhat and sun block
- Water bag (can be rolled up when I don't need it)
- Head torch and batteries
- Tent: a dome tent that stands freely and doesn't need pegging into the hard ground. (I'll mostly use just the netting part, so I can look up at the stars.)
- Medical kit

A few important additions:
- Two huge plastic boxes with lids to hold all food, plates, etc. Dustproof, I hope - but I'll also bag up everything in freezer bags.
- Two gigantic containers of water and a water bag. For two weeks I'm not sure that this will be enough ... may need another one or two?

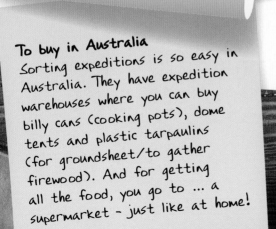

To buy in Australia
Sorting expeditions is so easy in Australia. They have expedition warehouses where you can buy billy cans (cooking pots), dome tents and plastic tarpaulins (for groundsheet/to gather firewood). And for getting all the food, you go to ... a supermarket - just like at home!

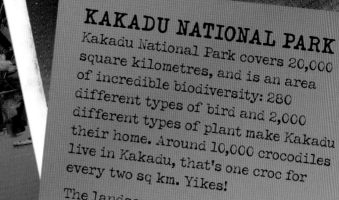

KAKADU NATIONAL PARK

Kakadu National Park covers 20,000 square kilometres, and is an area of incredible biodiversity: 280 different types of bird and 2,000 different types of plant make Kakadu their home. Around 10,000 crocodiles live in Kakadu, that's one croc for every two sq km. Yikes!

The landscape ranges from grassland, to freshwater wetlands (left) and even saltwater estuaries in the north. In the south, hills and ridges of ancient volcanic rock are separated by woodland areas.

PEMBROKE BRANCH TEL. 6689575

WEATHER

The Northern Territory experiences a tropical summer between November and March, and a dry season between April and October. Some areas of Kakadu National Park have to close during the summer due to flooding.

Northern Territory, Australia

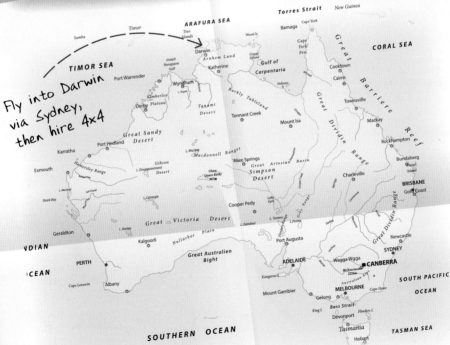

Fly into Darwin via Sydney, then hire 4x4

DRIVING THROUGH THE OUTBACK

It's going to be very hot, sunny and dry where I'm going, though there will be some rivers and swampy wetlands (crocodile infested). I'll be driving long distances, so I need to be prepared - see note below. MOST important - I will let people know where I'm going and when I expect to be back, AND if the car breaks down, I will stay with it. This is far safer that wandering through semi-desert and collapsing of dehydration. I plan to always have at least 10 litres of water in the back of the car.

Car kit
- Basic tool kit, jack and spare tyre (obviously!)
- Sand ladders and shovel (right) just in case the car gets stuck in soft sand

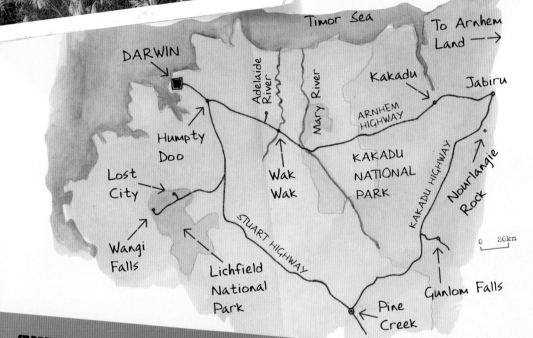

DARWIN

Timor Sea

To Arnhem Land →

Adelaide River

Mary River

Kakadu

Jabiru

ARNHEM HIGHWAY

Humpty Doo

Lost City

Wak Wak

KAKADU NATIONAL PARK

KAKADU HIGHWAY

Nourlangie Rock

Wangi Falls

Lichfield National Park

STUART HIGHWAY

0   20km

Gunlom Falls

Pine Creek

To Alice Springs

THE OUTBACK

My journey to Kakadu will take me through the dry and remote areas of the outback. A combination of grassland and desert biomes, the outback includes the vast remote interior of Australia, or the 'Red Centre' as it is sometimes known.

Arid and semi-arid desert lands make up 70 per cent of mainland Australia, where only three per cent of the total population lives. There are ten major Australian deserts, including the Tanami and Great Sandy deserts. A large proportion of desert land is owned by Aboriginal tribes – some of Australia's indigenous people.

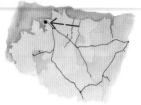

Arrived In Darwin!

I'm in the city of Darwin in Australia's 'top end' - the Northern Territory. I've flown here from Sydney.

North of here is the Timor Sea and then the islands of Indonesia, and everywhere to the south is outback. The next large town heading south is Alice Springs, which is close to Uluru, and that's 1,499 km away!

This place is INCREDIBLE.

They have a shop that's just made for me – a wilderness expedition outfitters. It's a warehouse full of rucksacks, bush-knives, assorted cooking gear and every piece of kit you could possibly need for 'going outback'. There's even a 'Mini Moke', which is like an old mini car but with the roof taken off and 'jeepified' for off-road use.

6

What a beaut,

as they say here in Oz. A white, long-wheel base Nissan Patrol, with high ground clearance and four-wheel drive. I've hired it for two weeks.

I have to get it back in the same condition, and I can go just about anywhere – but not the track to Jim Jim Falls. The people at the car hire office said the track would wreck the suspension and end up with someone having to come out to rescue me.

GRASSLANDS

Any areas outside of towns and cities with few inhabitants tend to be referred to by Australians as 'the bush'. This can be agricultural areas or open expanses of grassland. Grasslands are places with enough water for grasses to grow, but not enough to support many trees. Australia's grasslands are often teeming with insects, birds, reptiles and marsupials.

LATER...

After a trip to the supermarket to pick up all of my food, I'm heading south ...

Never-ending Roads

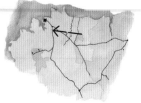

28 July

Just pulled off the highway for a break. (It's called the Stuart Highway - named after a guy who explored the centre of Australia.)

The rock and sand really are red.

It makes you realise how big the distances are around here. Just four hours in, and dry, dusty scrub stretches in all directions. In fact, the view has been roughly the same since leaving Darwin – and right now, I'm moving fast on a highway in good condition.

ALICE SPRINGS

Alice Springs is a remote town found in the south of Australia's Northern Territory. Aboriginal peoples have lived in the area for at least 30,000 years. It is a central point on the route from the north to the south of the country. It is now an important tourist centre for those wishing to explore the 'Red Centre' and for people wanting to visit Uluru.

ULURU

Uluru is a giant sandstone hill or mountain which rises up 348 m out of the red earth that surrounds it. Uluru began forming around 550 million years ago and is an important and sacred site for Aboriginal peoples. It is visited by around 250,000 people every year.

Road trains
are the vehicles I'm
scared of –

they are three-trailer juggernauts that ferry supplies down to Alice Springs. They get up to speed on the long straight highways and just keep going and going. Apparently they need about half a kilometre to stop – which is why, when they come steaming along behind me, I pull off onto the roadside verge. As they go past there's a huge gust of wind that rocks the car and sends up

clouds of dust and often a shower of gravel.

Farmed emus behind a stock fence.

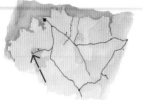

Time For A Break

I've been driving for miles. I've seen a couple of distant wallabies so far, a swooping kite and wedge-tailed eagles ... **plus lots of termite mounds*** – **everywhere!**

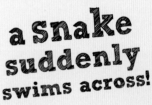

I stop at a campsite close to Wangi Falls in Litchfield National Park. There's a pool at the bottom of the waterfall where I join loads of people swimming when

a snake suddenly swims across!

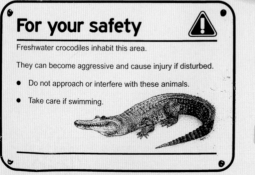

For your safety ⚠

Freshwater crocodiles inhabit this area.

They can become aggressive and cause injury if disturbed.

- Do not approach or interfere with these animals.
- Take care if swimming.

I didn't know what sort it was, but I certainly swam away fast. Nobody else did. Were they just less observant than me, or was this a safe, non-poisonous snake?

Signpost next to the falls.

* See pages 16–17.

There's loads of birdlife
around the campsite:

– Red-tailed black cockatoos
(Calyptorhynchus banksii) in
a tree above our camp spot
(top, right).

– A bowerbird that decorates
its display area (where it
impresses females) with colourful
pieces of litter – crisp packets,
sweet wrappers, etc.

– Blue-winged kookaburras
(Dacelo leachii, right) that
swoop into nick any food left
lying around. I was preparing
tonight's barbecue when it flew
off with one of the bread rolls.

SNAKES

There are many snake species
found in the Northern Territory.
Some snakes are non-venomous,
such as the golden tree snake,
while others are highly venomous,
such as the death adder (left) or
the black whip snake. They often
feed on small mammals, birds and
other reptiles and can be found
basking on rocks in the Sun or
in tree branches.

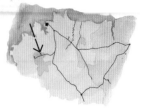

Weird Rock Formations

The plan is to drive up a little track to a set of rocky outcrops called the Lost City, in Litchfield National Park.
But it's not easy getting the 4x4 up here!

That was the roughest track

so far and the reason I hired a four-wheel drive. Most of it was just bumps down a dirt track through a forest of thin gum trees (eucalyptus), but in places the ground was really sandy. I made use of the mini gear stick just in front of the main one that puts the car into four wheel mode.*

This whole area is the remains of a sandstone escarpment, eroded by wind and rain over the years into knobbly rocks and pillars. When the route started to climb, there were big rock slabs and it was like driving up a set of stairs. At one narrow section there was a drop off to the side – just a metre or so, but if I had slipped, the car would have ended up with its wheels overhanging and

I've no idea how I would have got it back on the track.

* To save fuel I'm using two-wheel drive most of the time out on the road.

12

The rocks of the Lost City (left) feel like old ruins – mainly because the flat ground is sandy and the rocky outcrops stand up a bit like walls, sometimes with short arches or tunnels linking different 'rooms'.

There are short-eared rock-wallabies hanging round the cliffs of a deep and a very jungly gorge, not far down from a trail around the Lost City. We are on top of the plateau and everything up here is dry and faded-looking, but down in the gorge there are ferns and palms and bigger trees. That must mean there's permanent water down there.

SHORT-EARED ROCK-WALLABIES
(PETROGALE BRACHYOTIS)

The rocky areas around the gorge are a favourite habitat for the short-eared rock-wallaby. These little critters are found in the northern-most parts of the Northern Territory. They are marsupials, and have a dark stripe on their necks, with a white throat and belly. Short-eared rock-wallabies mainly feed on grasses, bark and roots.

13

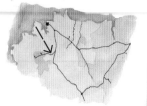

Camping

Someone back at Wangi Falls said there were fruit bats around here, so I went for a late afternoon walk after setting up camp. I didn't expect to find anything and ... **here we are!**

Little red flying foxes (*Pteropus scapulatus*) – I thought they would be hard to find, but there are masses of them dangling from the trees all around.

There's a **fruity poo smell** here.

Frilled lizard (*Chlamydosaurus kingii*) up a tree.

I spied a frilled lizard and was really hoping it would open its frill out to try to scare me away, or run away down the tree and across the ground on its hind feet, dinosaur-style. Instead, it just scurried further up the tree when it got annoyed at me trying to sketch it!

14

I'm driving through Litchfield on a dirt track that the map says will eventually lead back to the highway, and onto Kakadu.

There are loads of magnetic termite mounds around here. They are on seasonally flooded grassland, where the termites can't escape underground for cooling, so they build their homes above ground. The mounds look like gravestones in a cemetery. Most of them are lined up north to south.

In the morning, the termites go to the east-face where the Sun warms them up (the Sun rises in the east, obviously). At midday, they stay in the middle where it's cooler. The mound is edge-on to the Sun, so it doesn't get too hot. In the afternoon it's warmer on the west side.

Magnetic termite mounds make great nesting sites for hooded parrots (*Psephotellus dissimilis*, left), gorgeous sky-blue birds with dark heads, and also for quolls, which are small marsupial carnivores that look a bit like pointy-nosed cats. Goannas (big lizards), rats and snakes also live in termite mounds.

15

Termites!

Termites munch up wood and grass. Their soft white bodies dry out quickly in the Sun, so they stay in the cover of their mounds made of

dried mud which they have chewed up and spat out.

The termites near Litchfield National Park are wood termites (left), which are easy to find as all you have to do is break open just about any dead wood branch you find lying on the ground.

I presume the termites from the mounds look much the same, but I haven't tried breaking into any termite mounds to check this out. For a start, termite mounds are

concrete HARD,

but I also think breaking bits off one to see what's inside is too destructive.

16

- Tree piping termites are found at the base of trees. Half of all eucalyptus trees here have been hollowed out by termites.

- Cathedral termites (top left mound) live on dry land where it doesn't flood.

- Floodplain termites (bottom left mound) live in seasonally flooded grasslands and build large grey conical mounds.

Many termites just live underground with no visible nest.

DIDGERIDOO
These Aboriginal wind-instruments were traditionally made from logs hollowed out by termites. To play a didgeridoo, you mould a strip of beeswax into a sausage-shape and wrap it in a ring around one end of the tube to make a sort of mouthpiece. I can get a low, droning trumpeting out of my didgeridoo, but not for very long. You are meant to do something called circular breathing to keep the notes going on and on, but I can't work out how to do it.

I bought this didgeridoo at a craft shop on the edge of Darwin, at the end of my trip.

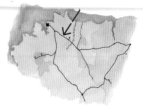

Bushfires

(Yes, there really is a place called 'Humpty Doo', or at least there are signposts to it.)

I can spy swooping black kites (*Milvus migrans* left) at the edge of a recent bushfire, hunting (I presume) for small animals flushed out by the flames. Black kites follow bushfires and even spread them by picking up burning sticks and dropping them to keep the fire burning forwards.

Nature finds ways to survive, despite the bushfire.

An agile wallaby flees the area and the charcoal-blackened stump of a cabbage palm will eventually re-grow. By peeling the charred bark at the base of a gum tree trunk, I can see that the tree is fine underneath.

EUCALYPTUS TREES

Three-quarters of native Australian forests are made up of eucalyptus trees (gum trees). These trees are perfectly adapted to nutrient-poor soils and drought. They have numerous ways of recovering from bushfires. The majority of eucalyptus trees are evergreen, so they keep their oil-rich leaves all year round.

There are also cycads, a family of plants that has been around since the **days of the dinosaurs!**

CYCADS

Cycads (right) have a short, woody trunk, with large, stiff evergreen leaves sprouting from the top. They are found in tropical and sub-tropical parts of the world. Some types of cycad prefer wet rainforest conditions, while others can survive in harsh desert areas, growing in sand or rock.

The cycads look a bit charred, like the other plants in this burned patch, but I think many of them are adapted to bushfires sweeping past. The foliage will grow back and new seedlings will sprout up out of the ground.

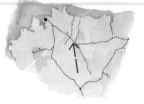

Nearly At Kakadu

There's a huge wetland area on the way into Kakadu. Wide and open with lagoons edged with lily pads –

a real contrast to the **dry open woodland and grassland** I have been driving through.

There are vast amounts of wetland birds in the marshland; mainly pied herons, egrets, magpie geese and white ibis (*Threskiornis molucca*, left). There are whistling kites

swooping

around everywhere (see right).

Spotted some sort of goanna sitting on the causeway road. I didn't even notice it at first, as I was so busy looking at birds through my binoculars. I think it crept up on me.

It must be about 1.5 metres long!

20

GOANNAS

Around 25 of the 30 species of goanna lizard live in Australia. They are often quite large, with some species growing to 2.5 m in length. The goanna preys on any animal small enough for it to catch, including small mammals, other lizards, snakes and birds. Some species spend most of their time in trees, while others enjoy living in swampy areas.

WHISTLING KITES
(HALIASTUR SPHENURUS)

This bird of prey produces a call, sounding like a whistle, as it flies overhead or when perched in a tree. It has a light-brown head with dark-brown wings, and a wingspan of 120 cm to 145 cm. It is found across Australia, in woodlands, across grasslands, but most often in wetlands. It feeds on dead animals or preys on rabbits, hares, fish, reptiles and birds.

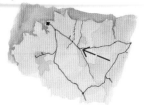

Outside Kakadu N. P.

1 AUG, 7.30 PM, Mary River campsite

Still outside Kakadu National Park here, but the wildlife is **abundant!**

Eucalyptus trees close to the Mary River campsite.

Seen lots of wallabies and buffalo already, and there is a network of rough tracks between billabongs (waterholes) which will be worth exploring for a day or two. Mike, who runs the campsite where I'm staying, took me for a quick drive out there this afternoon and, with the map he lent me, I reckon I can work out a route around the billabongs, eucalyptus woodland and grassy plains that I can drive myself tomorrow.

Morning drive

I've found some antilopine wallaroos (Macropus antilopinus), most of them are hopping away fast.

Their tails go up when their legs go forwards and go down when their legs go back. Wallaroo's are small kangaroos, bigger than wallabies but not as big as the huge red kangaroos, which live further south in the drier scrub.

BILLABONG

A billabong is the name Australians give to an oxbow lake – a pool of water left behind when a river changes course. The billabongs around here are shrinking as it's the dry season. Each one is surrounded by cracked, dried-up mud. Further in lies slimy green weed, with clearer water in the centre. During the wet season, the billabongs fill again, providing a freshwater source for wildlife.

I've been walking round a bit with my binoculars, bird and wallaby spotting, but I must admit I never go too near to the water or to the pandanus (screw pine, see page 24) thickets as Mike warned me about saltwater crocodiles.

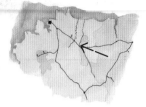

Mary River

Four-wheel drive!

Hardies Creek is one of five rivers that the Mary River splits into as a delta. All the rivers here head northwards towards the sea. The further north you get, the swampier conditions become. There are lots of small channels, which I suppose all get joined together when the place floods in the wet season.

SCREW PINE
(PANDANUS SPIRALIS)
Screw pine is found on the banks of rivers, billabongs and streams and around coastal areas of northern Australia. It is a shrub or small tree, which can grow to 10 m tall. Screw pines are so-called because of the way their spiny leaves corkscrew upwards.

24

FRESHWATER CROCODILES
(CROCODYLUS JOHNSONI)

I've spied freshwater crocs along the river. These grow to about 3 m and can live for up to 50 years! They enjoy a diet of fish, insects and crustaceans, and can be found in freshwater billabongs, rivers, creeks and wetlands. They have narrower snouts and are smaller AND FAR LESS DANGEROUS than saltwater crocs!

I went through a half-dried up river to get here.

Real four-wheel drive stuff.

There was only a trickle of water, but I had to drive down a steep bank which was angled sideways, so it felt that the 4x4 might roll.

At the bottom there was deep mud. The 4x4 had a sticky moment where I thought I'd become stuck. But, I kept the engine revs high and powered up the mud bank on the other side.

LATER...

Now I have to do the whole journey in reverse to get back to camp ...

Outback

2 AUG, 8 PM, Mary River campsite

I've just seen this little fella in the leaf litter, before it climbed a palm tree next to the car.

He's got a cream and red-brown checkerboard pattern and must be about 70 cm long.

Brown tree snake

3 AUG, outback near Mary River

There's an Australian bustard (Ardeotis australis) striding through the grassland.

Not far beyond, I glimpse some feral buffalo. I have also seen wild pigs and wild horses: escapees from people's farms that went wild long ago.

SALTY CROCS
(CROCODYLUS POROSUS)
Saltwater crocodiles are the big, mean crocodiles around here. Though they can live in saltwater, around the coast, they are more often found in rivers. Salty crocs grow huge and **they can kill people.**

Eighty per cent of a saltwater crocodile's diet is crab, twenty per cent is large animals, such as buffalo, fish, birds and even fruit bats.
To hunt, they spot their prey, submerge in water (which they can do for up to one hour!) and then

PEMBROKE BRANCH TEL. 6689575

strike!

They have a closable flap of skin at the back of their mouth to stop water going down when they swallow food.

There are more wallaroos around here,

plus some agile wallabies (*Macropus agilis*). These wallabies have an eye stripe and a thigh stripe on their coats, and they're a bit smaller than wallaroos.

27

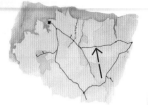

The Park

4 AUG, Kakadu

Following the Arnhem Highway, which leads
to the Yolngu territory of Arnhem Land,
I arrive at Kakadu National Park.

At first, it doesn't look any different here to all the outback that I have
already driven through.

The petrol stop of Jabiru (named after the big storks that live here) is about
as far as most people get to. There are blobby orange sandstone escarpments
with wetlands in between.

I'm planning to see some **ancient Aboriginal rock art**

and to take a boat trip on one of the lagoons, before heading southwards
in the 4x4 to a remote set of waterfalls at the edge of the park.

28

Nourlangie Rock

There is Aboriginal art in the overhangs of the cliffs. This painting (below) is ancient, although I think it's been redrawn, or at least outlined, at various times over the years. I think these are pictures of The Dreaming. The 'paint' is chalk, or red and yellow ochre (rocks with iron oxide in).

INDIGENOUS PEOPLE

Aboriginal peoples, together with the Torres Strait Islander peoples, are indigenous peoples of Australia. They have lived in Australia for 45,000 to 50,000 years, long before Europeans settled in the 1700s. Aboriginal peoples' Dreaming stories pass on important knowledge and values. They tell of Ancestor Spirits that came to earth and created the land, animals and plants, before transforming into other objects, including the stars.

This picture is called 'X-ray style'. There are some other pictures that show the arrival of Europeans hunting buffalo, and one shows a sailing ship. Others are said to show thylacines (Tasmanian 'wolves'), which became extinct here 3,500 years ago.

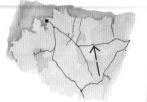

Boat Trip

Green ant nest

This green ant (or weaver ant) is a great source of protein and fatty acids. Green ants are found across Australia. **The green abdomen is acid, tangy lemon flavour. I've tried it twice now.**

(You bite off the ant's bum!)

The ants' nests are made of dead leaves, joined up with white silk made by the ant larvae. I was told you can boil up the nests to make medicinal tea, and you can boil up the ants (with sugar ... of course) to make jam.

Scribbly gums?

I think this eucalyptus tree might be a 'scribbly gum', so named because of the patterns on the bark which are caused by moth caterpillars underneath.

It's the crack of dawn and surprisingly cool. The mist is rising over the wetlands.

There are thousands of plumed whistling ducks on the water, and v-shaped skeins of magpie geese flying overhead (left). Nankeen night heron are abundant here and the black-necked jabiru sweeps its bill back and forth through the water snapping up food with a

very vigorous swishing movement.

There are pink lotus flowers with big round leaves that dangle clear of the water. I've also seen a jacana, or lily trotter bird, with long toes that spread its weight over the lily pads so it doesn't sink through. Strange to think, in amongst all these thousands of birds there will be

salty crocs lurking under the water ...

JABIRU (EPHIPPIORHYNCHUS ASIATICUS)

Black-necked storks are commonly called 'jabirus' in Australia. They are tall, long-necked storks, with black and white feathers and a large black bill. They are secretive birds, which inhabit wetland areas and feed on fish, crabs and frogs.

This is a male jabiru.

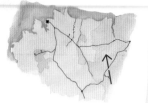

Starry Night

5 AUG, carrying on south

I stop on the Jim Jim falls track. I've only driven a short way up it, and it looks much the same as all the other dirt tracks around here.

I am tempted to carry on as I would love to explore the falls. BUT ...

... not driving this track was part of the agreement when I hired this vehicle. Can it really be that bad? I guess I won't find out ... **so, onto the next set of waterfalls: Gunlom.**

I've camped just off the road. The stars are fantastic, with the sky totally black and very, very clear. Just found the constellation of 'Scorpio' and it does look like a scorpion. Shooting stars and a satellite crossed the sky.

I've made my campfire quite small – just enough to boil up some pasta. All the wood I pick up is hollowed out by termites, and so dry that it lights instantly (setting fire to it sends termites streaming out).

I've scraped away all the dry eucalyptus leaves so that there is bare sand all around my fire, but still I'm worried about sparks setting off a bushfire.

It really is so dry around here and ready to burn!

LATER...

I pulled out the burning logs and covered each with sand. I'm sleeping out tonight on top of my dome tent, which I'm using without the poles as a ground sheet.

THE SOUTHERN CROSS

The Southern Cross is one of the most distinctive and visible star constellations found in the southern hemisphere. It is made up of five stars, which form a cross-shape in the night sky. The Southern Cross is found on the Australian flag: one small five-pointed star and four larger seven-pointed stars.

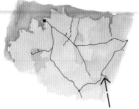

Gunlom Falls

Doves cooing, **screeching** parrots?

There's a line of termites snuggled under my sleeping bag this morning. Breakfast is leftover pasta and soup. I don't want to risk another fire.

4 PM

So dusty!

Red dust is ingrained into my skin, so I look lined and old. My hair is stiff with dust! The lesson learned: close the windows and use the 4x4 air con when you're driving down dirt roads.

PARROTS

There are roughly 375 parrot species in the world, with 56 of these found in Australia. The red-winged parrot is found in northern and northeastern parts of the country in forest areas and along rivers. These parrots have beautiful green feathers, and red and black wings.

It's been quite a journey getting here,

most of it on dirt roads over and around scrubby ridges, through forests of gum trees and down to a wide, green river's edge. I suppose you could call it a valley, but it's basically just a flat area between blocky ridges, one of which has a narrow waterfall tumbling down it to a wide pool with reeds and tall white-barked trees around the edge.

34

This is the view from the top of Gunlom Falls.
Scrubby ridges stretch endlessly into the distance.

Kakadu and the wetlands are to the north. In fact, the river in
the valley below where the water from Gunlom Falls flows, is the
Mary River. It eventually leads to the wetlands where I was a few
days ago. To the south (left of the picture above), there really
is nothing. It gets drier and flatter, and becomes desert.

The warden of the campsite
at the base of the falls said

**there's a track that
heads south from here,**

but if I drive down it I should
tell him when I'm setting off
and when I plan to get back.
The track leads to an old uranium
mine, but it's really remote and
the chance of rescue is unlikely
if no one knows you are there.
The journey up will take a whole
day. So I will stay the night at
the mine before heading back.

Gunlom Falls

River Crossing

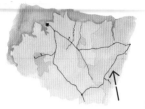

Mating snakes?....
or are they fighting?

The snakes are plain and grey brown, which means they could be mulga snakes, king brown snakes or taipans. All of these species are deadly poisonous, so I'm not getting out for a closer look. Engine off and wait ...

**That took a surprising amount of time:
10–15 minutes before the snakes moved away!**

On track. Close to the uranium mine.

That has quite shaken me up. I got the car stuck in a river. This is why I should have hired a 4x4 with a snorkel! The river looked really shallow. In fact, I had crossed it several times before; easy scrunching across wet gravel with water not even up to the axles.

Third time unlucky!

The track went down more of a bank that time. I lined up, pushed the mini gearstick into four-wheel mode and kept the revs up as I went into the water, which was just as well. The water went straight up to the headlights and the front was still tilting slightly downwards. The exhaust pipe was well under water and I knew that whatever, in these situations, you have to keep the revs up.

The uranium mine

If you don't keep pumping out exhaust, the exhaust pipe can suck back water and the engine stops.

Panic moment!

Should I slam the car into reverse and back out? No! I had to keep the revs up. So I carried on forward, stopped as I must've hit some submerged rock with the front tyres, then almost bounced back up as the tyres gripped it and the wheels pulled over the rock. I was still in the middle of the river though and the water was alongside the doors.

LATER ...

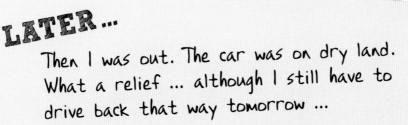

Then I was out. The car was on dry land. What a relief ... although I still have to drive back that way tomorrow ...

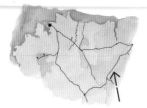

The Mine

I must admit I was a bit scared the Nissan might die if I let the engine stop, so I drove on for about another hour.

So here I am, camped by a stand of eucalyptus trees close to the river (which is just a tiny stream here). There are a few tracks leading off into the bush. The plan is to explore around tomorrow before heading back to Gunlom Falls.

8 AUG, morning walk

I saw a few more agile wallabies on my walk around the mine area, also a couple of larger kangaroos in the distance.

I'd like to think these are red kangaroos, the biggest type, but they're more likely to be antilopine kangaroos. There were sulphur crested cockatoos and emus (left). A pair of them, long-legged, picking their way through tufty, light-green grass.

I tried to follow them to get a closer look. They just walked away while I got my legs spiked on the grass which, close-up, was like tufts of green porcupine quills.
It might be spinifex grass.

SPINIFEX GRASS

Spinifex (above) is famously tough and spiky. This grass is found over much of the desert sand and rocky ranges of the 'Red Centre'. It thrives on poor, dry soil by sending its roots down a long way to get water: approximately 3 m. Spinifex leaves are tough and indigestible to most animals, except termites.

KANGAROOS

Kangaroos are found in grasslands, rocky slopes and some forest areas. They feed on grass, fruit and seeds. Kangaroos tend to be bigger than wallabies. A red kangaroo (left) can grow to 2 m tall and weigh as much as 90 kg. All kangaroos have short hair, powerful hind legs, big feet and long tails. They can reach speeds of 60 kph and can clear 8 m in a single bound!

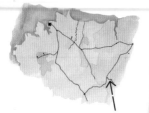

Back To Gunlom Falls

I've been dreading this, but scouting around it now looks so much easier.

It seems there are two river crossings: the one where I nearly bogged down and another 15 m or so further on.

It looks flatter but I'm going to test out the way first by wading in with a stick and prodding the river bed in front.

There are no salty crocs here

– I checked yesterday with Mark, the campsite man.

5 minutes later!

Well, that was easy!

The second way across was much flatter and the water barely went up to the top of the wheels. It came up over the exhaust pipe, but I kept the revs up and I sloshed forwards nicely.

40

DINGOES

Dingoes are a type of wild dog believed to have been introduced to Australia about 40,000 years ago. They have a ginger or sandy coat and can grow to 60 cm tall and 35 kg in weight. Dingoes prey on mammals, birds and reptiles.

Just seen a dingo, close to the falls. Mark, the Lancashire camp warden, said dingoes are still common around here – unlike quolls (see page15) which are dying out because they keep trying to eat cane toads.

CANE TOADS (RHINELLA MARINA)

Cane toads come from South America. In fact, I've seen them in the Amazon where they are not a problem. They were introduced into Queensland in the 1930s to kill beetles that were eating sugar cane. The trouble is, cane toads are poisonous to eat, killing native animals, such as quolls and goannas, that normally eat frogs.

LATER...

I'm starting to pack up my gear, as I head off north early tomorrow morning, back towards Darwin ...

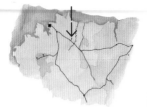

Adelaide River

Crocodile jumping trip!

On the way back to Darwin now and going on a touristy boat trip to see jumping crocodiles.

They are huge...

and I'm glad I'm on a big boat with railings between me and them. A guy on the top deck dangles a steak on the end of a pole and the crocs jump up to get it. We are talking seriously high jumping. There are also other crocs too big to bother jumping.

The old male above was 6 metres long. He's very black (and olive mottled). He's probably over a hundred years old.

Huge and scary!

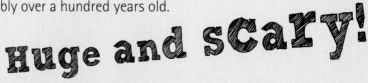

This is what it must be like to meet a dinosaur.

From here, the Adelaide River and the Mary River (which isn't far to the east) wind their way northwards to the Timor Sea. On my map the rivers are just shown as blue dashed lines because every November they change their courses when the rainy season hits.

ADELAIDE RIVER

This river flows north from Brock's Creek to Adam Bay and into the Timor Sea. It is 180 km long and it is well-known for the number of saltwater crocodiles in its waters. White-bellied sea eagles and whistling kites can also be found here.

In a few months the rivers will burst their banks and everywhere turns into a huge swampy lake. This is the time of the year when crocodiles have been known to turn up in the middle of Darwin! Now, in August, it's the middle of the dry season, the rivers are flowing down this year's channels and the crocodiles are all along them and easy to see.

LATER...

Fuel stop for journey back ...

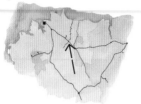

Wak Wak

I've stopped somewhere called Wak Wak (a place, not the noise a duck makes!). I'm about to start the long drive back to Darwin.

It's all highways now with no exciting off-road bits. Amazingly the car has survived unscratched and I'm hoping there will be no passing road trains to pelt the paintwork with gravel on the way back.

Wak Wak is still very much in the outback.

There are five buildings and a

concrete crocodile, painted green.

Then there are just gum trees, fields of termite mounds and wetlands pretty much all the way to Humpty Doo when I pick up the main Stuart Highway. This will be my last chance to see wallabies and the big-horned feral buffalo that sometimes hang-out in the marshy bits alongside the roads.

DARWIN

Darwin is the capital city of the Northern Territory. It is located on the northern most tip, next to the Timor Sea. Darwin is a tourist hub for those wanting to explore Kakadu and the 'Red Centre'. It has a tropical climate with wet and dry seasons and it is particularly prone to cyclones during the wet season. The city had to be almost entirely rebuilt three times between 1897 and 1974 after devastating cyclones.

I washed that car until it was gleaming, swept out all the dust. It turns out that I needn't have bothered. All the guy at the car hire place could say was:

'Looks like you didn't get to have any fun in it – we'd let you off a few knocks, you know!'

On The Beach

13 AUG, Sydney, on Manly beach having a barbecue You only realise quite how huge Australia is when it takes four hours to fly across it. I'm now back in Sydney - flying back to the UK tomorrow.

Australia is not just a country - it's a continent - and sitting on the beach surrounded by people, it makes me realise just how wild the Northern Territory is, and remember how vulnerable humans can be in tough environments. I'll take some fantastic memories away with me: driving through miles of outback scrub and off-roading through wetlands and up rocky escarpments. But it's the wildlife that I'll remember the most: the deadly snakes, bounding kangaroos and crocodiles.

The wildlife is everywhere - even on Manly Beach! A kookaburra has just swooped onto the picnic table I'm sitting at and taken one of my sausages!

ARNHEM LAND

The wilderness of rocky escarpments and swampy wetlands continues past Kakadu National Park into the vast north-eastern corner of Australia's Northern Territory. Arnhem Land is home to the Yolngu people and other Aboriginal tribes who have lived here for thousands of years, and permits are needed for visitors to enter. There are many sacred sites with intricate rock paintings showing the Ancestor Spirits of The Dreaming.

The ancient paintings have been re-coloured in with each new generation. Other pictures show more recent events, like the arrival of Europeans in sailing ships and modern aeroplanes.

Glossary

arid Having little or no rain, very dry.

billabong A pool of water formed after a river changes its course.

biodiversity The variety of plant and animal life on planet Earth.

bushfire An uncontrolled fire that burns in grass, bush or woodland.

conical Having the shape of a cone.

constellations A group of stars in the sky which form a recognisable pattern when viewed from Earth.

crustacean An animal with a hard outer shell, which often lives in water, such as a crab.

cyclone A tropical storm in which the wind moves in a circular motion.

dehydration The loss or removal of water to harmful levels.

delta (river) A landform created when small pieces of earth and rock (sediment) is deposited as a river flows into slower water.

eroded To have gradually worn away through the action of weather or waves.

escarpment A cliff-like ridge of land.

estuary The wide part of a river where it meets the sea and freshwater mixes with saltwater.

feral Wild, not owned or controlled.

gorge A deep, narrow valley with steep sides, often formed when a river cuts between two areas of hard rock.

Indigenous To have originally come from a particular place.

lagoon An area of saltwater separated from the sea by a reef or bank of sand.

larvae Plural of larva, the form of an insect or animal before it becomes an adult, such as a caterpillar.

marshland An area of land that remains waterlogged for much of the year, often found at the edges of lakes or streams.

marsupial A type of mammal where babies are carried in a pouch on the adults' stomach.

native A person born and strongly linked to a specific place.

nutrient A substance an animal or plant needs to live and grow.

sandstone A type of rock formed mainly of sand grains and quartz.

southern hemisphere The part of Earth lying south of the equator.

tarpaulin A tough, waterproof material or cloth.

Franklin Watts
First published in Great Britain in 2018 by
The Watts Publishing Group

Copyright © The Watts Publishing Group 2018

All rights reserved

Executive editor: Adrian Cole
Series designer: Elaine Wilkinson
Design manager: Peter Scoulding
Picture researcher: Diana Morris

Photo acknowledgements:

All illustrations and photos S. Chapman except: Adwo/Shutterstock: 7c. Baldas1950/Shutterstock: 33b. ronny bas/Shutterstock: 39t. Australian Camera/Shutterstock: 30b. Sean Burges/Alamy: 46t. John Carnemolla/Shutterstock: 13c. Blue Jacaranda/Shutterstock: 33c. Daniela Constantinescu/Shutterstock: 5t. Craig R-AU/Shutterstock: 21b, 37t, 39b. charnsitr/Shutterstock: 2c, 25t, 29c. Epoch Catcher/Shutterstock: 42c. Factoryhill/Alamy: 20c. Ecoprint/Shutterstock: 10b. Susan Flashman/Shutterstock: 34t. Halfpoint/Shutterstock: 47t. Ecoprint/Shutterstock: 46-47bg, 48bg. Hemis/Alamy: 1tr, 47b. Mark Higgins/Shutterstock: 1bg, 2-3bg, 4-5bg, Chris Ison/Shutterstock: 24b. Emma Jones/Shutterstock: 43c. Inge Hogenbijl/Shutterstock: 9b. Lesniewski/Shutterstock: 3b. LOOK Die Bildagenteur der Fotografen GmbH/Alamy: 45b. Steve Lovegrove/Shutterstock: 6c, 45t. Jacqui Martin/Shutterstock: 35b. Henrik Larsson/Shutterstock: 13c. Rainer Isabelle van Mierlo/Shutterstock: 3b. Mr F/Shutterstock: all palm fronds. Maurizio de Mattei/Shutterstock: 1br, Panther Media GmbH /Alamy: 44t. Pichit Sansupa/Shutterstock: 41c. National Geographic Creative/Alamy: 13b. 13t. snapcraft/Shutterstock: 19t. Chris Watson/Shutterstock: 16c. Phillip Schubert/Shutterstock: 44b. Tim Whitby/Alamy: 46c.

Every attempt has been made to clear copyright. Should there be any inadvertent omission please apply to the publisher for rectification.

ISBN 978 1 4451 5684 2

Printed in China

Franklin Watts
An imprint of Hachette Children's Group
Part of The Watts Publishing Group
Carmelite House
50 Victoria Embankment
London EC4Y 0DZ

An Hachette UK Company
www.hachette.co.uk

www.franklinwatts.co.uk

MIX
Paper from responsible sources
FSC® C104740
www.fsc.org

CHERYL COLE

PROMISE

FACTFILE

Birthplace: Newcastle upon Tyne, England

Previous job: waitress

Been singing since: age 12

Favourite book: *The Twits* by Roald Dahl

Favourite film: *Ghost*

Full name: Cheryl Ann Cole

Old surname: Tweedy

Chinese star sign: pig

Favourite actor: George Clooney

Favourite food: Chinese takeaway

Favourite drink: vitamin water

Fears and phobias: cotton wool and flour on top of buns

Best presents received: a leather bag and a white-gold bracelet

Birthday: 30th June, 1983

Star sign: Cancer

Bad habits: leaving the bathwater in

First ever single bought: Rick Astley – 'Never Gonna Give You Up'

First ever concert seen: Steps

Random fact: Cheryl is a vegetarian

Favourite TV show: MTV reality TV series *The Hills*

Eye colour: brown

Hair colour: brown

Married: Yes, to hubby Ashley Cole (footballer)

Tattoos: our Chezza has five tattoos, a butterfly on her lower back, a ring of roses, leaves and musical notes around her thigh, a symbol on her hand, the words 'Mrs C' on the back of her neck, and a cheeky design on her bum!

"Whenever I get around the paparazzi, I get this nervous thing. I start to giggle."

Cheryl on the pap

Favourite colour: yellow

"Cheryl's strong, but she's also a softie and she doesn't realise how much people genuinely do love her."

Girls Aloud bandmate Kimberley Walsh

Cheryl's team: Sundraj Sreenivasan, Girls Aloud's PR spokesperson since they started, Lily her PA (and Girls Aloud's former PA – the band have to find a new one now), two stylists, Victoria Adcock (who also dresses Posh and Christina Aguilera) and Frank Strachan, and Girls Aloud manager, Hillary Shaw, former manager of Bananarama.

Awards!

Cheryl has won countless awards, including Britain's Most Inspirational Woman, UK's Fantasy Body, MTV UK's Favourite Celebrity of 2008, and Best Smile!

MEET CHERYL

The story of Cheryl Cole is a real rags-to-riches tale, of a talented girl born into poverty, who managed to dance and sing her way into the big time! Born Cheryl Ann Tweedy on a poor estate in Newcastle, this northern beauty has come a long way from the days of shabby trainers, cheap tracksuits and gelled-back hair!

From Boots bonniest baby to the first member of chart sensations Girls Aloud, today the stunning brunette has been voted the best-dressed woman on the planet more than once. She's a style icon and the whole nation looks to her closet for what fashions are rocking.

After her difficult 2007, she won our sympathy. Then as a judge on *X Factor 2008*, she took her place in our hearts as the kindest, most down-to-earth celebrity – a true princess of pop. With such a caring nature – the sweet singer even battled altitude sickness and climbed Mount Kilimanjaro to raise money for Comic Relief – is it any wonder we love her so much? With plans to conquer America and then the world, one thing is for sure – our Cheryl is going up and up!

Cheryl — Animal lover

There's no doubt that Cheryl's got a big heart, especially when it comes to animals. A lifetime lover of dogs, Chezza's pet chihuahua Buster is her best friend. "I see dogs as my babies," she says. "Sometimes I think I love dogs more than I love humans. I know they can't talk back to me. But they express their personalities in other ways. When I've been away for a couple of days Buster goes in a huff with me. He won't run up and be happy to see me – he'll give me a filthy look."

Cheryl's poochy keeps her grounded too. "I'll get home and Buster will have chewed off a Jimmy Choo heel or wet the floor. And he'll look at me as if to say, 'And what?' They bring me back down to earth."

Animal cruelty makes Chezza very sad indeed. "People see a newborn puppy and fall in love with it, she says, "but they don't have time to look after it properly. That's distressing enough. But to see cruelty breaks my heart."

"You're not supposed to have too much dairy because it can affect your voice, but I just couldn't resist it. Oh my God, it's heaven"

Cheryl on her fav treat, banoffee pie

THE FAIRYTALE

There was never a more romantic rags-to-riches fairytale than the story of Cheryl Cole. Born Cheryl Tweedy, Cheryl grew up on a poor Newcastle estate with her family: painter/decorator dad Gary, mum Joan, brothers Garry, Andrew and Joseph, sister Gillian and a half-sister called Mercedes.

But Cheryl was always destined for a future as a star. After winning competitions like Boots bonniest baby, Best Looking Girl of Newcastle, World Star Of The Future modelling contest, and Most Attractive Girl at the MetroCentre, Cheryl must have realised she was made for the big time!

In 2002, at the tender age of 19, she was the first girl chosen on TV talent show *Popstars: The Rivals* to join girl band, Girls Aloud. The group has become one of the most successful British pop groups, with 20 consecutive top 10 singles – including four number ones – and five platinum albums. In June 2008, Cheryl was chosen to replace Sharon Osbourne as a judge on *X Factor*, where she mentored the winning act, singer Alex Burke, and won our hearts in the process.

In 2008, Cheryl was named the celebrity that women would most like to be their best friend. According to the responses, Cheryl would make a great best friend. She might be a famous singer and TV star, but she still comes across as being a normal girl you could have a good night out and gossip with.

Q: How would Cheryl describe herself in three words?
A: Funny, Caring & Emotional

9

LIFE
BEFORE FAME

When you see her, with her footballer husband and her designer clothes, judging acts on *X Factor*, it's hard to imagine Cheryl came from such a tough background. It's even more difficult to remember that just a few years ago, as a nervous teenager, Cheryl was competing against other young hopefuls trying to impress judges on *Popstars: The Rivals*.

Cheryl has her family to thank for keeping her humble about her success – even from the beginning. "My mam would take me to auditions. If I got a part, Dad would shout, 'Get in there', but all Mam would say was, 'Oh, good.' She will always keep my feet on the ground," Cheryl says.

Cheryl's mum Joan remembers her daughter having great ambitions from the tender age of four years old! "She went to shopping centres all over the place, strutting her stuff on catwalks and stages," her mum spills.

"She has always wanted to be a star. She didn't want to do anything else. Nothing else would have satisfied her."

Star sign: Cancer

Born under the Cancer sign, Cheryl is **energetic** and **hard working**, with a philosophical view on life. Cancerians find it easy to tune in to others, which can inspire sympathetic understanding. Cancerians are very prone to be ruled by their feelings, and are affected by their environment and over-imaginative by nature. Sometimes Cancerians can live in the past.

11

POOR BEGINNINGS

Although she's wrapped in designer goodies these days, as a kid, the estate bully would tease Cheryl for wearing second-hand clothes. "She would give them to me herself when she was finished with them and then laugh when she'd see me clunking down the street in shoes stuffed with tissue paper because they were always too big," Cheryl says.

If she ever wanted to buy her own clothes, Cheryl did what all girls on her estate did – she got a loan from the 'Provi man'. "You know," she says, "the man from the Provident who'd come knocking on your door and ask if you needed to borrow some money. And then you'd take yourself down to River Island or Topshop and pay him back weekly," she says. The family weren't well off either:

"We didn't have any privileges. I remember living on baked beans and egg and bread – if it wasn't out of date," Cheryl continues. *"If we got a McDonald's or a Chinese takeaway, that was a treat, a luxury, because it was costing my mother a fortune."*

Cheryl – On the bad times in life

"Life's not easy. Life's not a bowl of cherries. Nobody's life is. And nobody's life ever will be. And I would hate to be one of those people that sail through life like that. Untested. Untouched. You're not living then: you're existing. You've got to experience the good and the bad in life – it's part of your character and makes you how you are."

For her 18th birthday, Cheryl went as a treat to an all-you-can-eat £5 Chinese buffet. But the family always supported her ambitions. "There wasn't a lot of money but Mam and Dad always found enough for my audition outfits," she says. "I was the show-off in the family."

In 1990, when she was seven, she made an advert for British Gas, and at ten, she joined the Newcastle Dance Centre, performing on Michael Barrymore's show *My Kind of People*.

When she was just nine years old, our Chez beat more than 5000 other dancers for a place at London's Royal Ballet Summer School. Her parents couldn't afford the £300 needed to send her to London for the summer, so a local paper did a story on her and the readers raised the money! But when she got there, Cheryl hated it! "I wanted to go home straight away," she says. "Everyone was prim and proper and I was just a Geordie from a council estate. It shattered my dream, but I didn't want to have to stand a certain way all my life and only eat salad."

By the age of 12, she was signed up by a management company and she returned to the Dance Centre in her teens to have routines choreographed, and then she started singing solo to shoppers at the MetroCentre in Gateshead. I wonder if any of them suspected that the girl who was singing was destined for such a bright future!

TOUGH TIMES

But things were sometimes hard. Cheryl grew up on an estate in Heaton, in Newcastle upon Tyne, where drugs and crime were a big problem. She lost one of her close friends to drugs in 2005, and has been an anti-drugs campaigner since, and some time in the future wants to set up a support network for families affected by drugs. Cheryl says: "It wasn't unhappy but it was tough, very tough. It's not really until the last couple of years I've realised it wasn't as easy as a lot

of people have it, but I'm not ashamed of it and I don't regret anything."

Her home life was tough too. When he was 13, her brother Andrew started to get into trouble with the police. And although Cheryl was top in performing arts, she struggled at school. "I was awful," she says. "They used to throw me out of class." Cheryl was the class clown – when the teachers called out the register, Cheryl would answer her name by saying "Mickey Mouse" or other silly things. But her former headmaster at Walker Comprehensive in Newcastle – Dr Steve Gaiter – remembers Cheryl more for being ambitious and talented: "Her passions were singing and dancing. But we didn't anticipate how big she would become. She stood head and shoulders above everybody else. She loved being centre stage."

BIG DREAMS

When she left school, Cheryl worked at a café, as a waitress on a floating nightclub, and toured the pub and club circuit before auditioning for TV talent show *Popstars: The Rivals* in 2002 – the event that changed her life.

"I am who I am because of what I went through and I'm just grateful for what I've achieved."

Cheryl

On *Popstars: The Rivals*, Cheryl was the first contestant to be picked for the group that would become Girls Aloud. The judges – Spice Girl Geri Halliwell, *X Factor* judge Louis Walsh and music producer Pete Waterman – were blown away by her. Pete Waterman fell in love with Cheryl at first sight, saying to her: "I think you have the most beautiful eyes and skin I've ever seen."

POPSTARS

Popstars: The Rivals was a 2002 TV talent show, where five girls who didn't know each other were picked to form a group, and went head to head against a group of boys, also put together on the show. The two groups were to compete for the UK Christmas Number 1 record. Given that this was how Girls Aloud were formed, no one expected them to last as long as they have, nor be as successful!

POPSTARS: THE SHOW

Thousands and thousands of hopefuls applied for the show, but after a long audition process, it was whittled down to just ten girls and ten guys who were to appear in front of the judges. During October and November 2002, the finalists took part in weekly live performances, and the public phoned in to vote for their favourites – the performers with the fewest votes were eliminated.

The girls who made it into the group were – in this order – Cheryl, Nicola, Nadine, Kimberley and Sarah. But Nicola and Kimberley almost didn't make it into the final ten – they

> "I remember her walking in on *Popstars: The Rivals*. She didn't have any confidence, but she connected with the public and she got the vote. She wasn't as beautiful as she is now, but she has come on a million miles."
>
> *Louis Walsh on Cheryl's early days*

were only recalled after two contestants pulled out at the last minute. Phew!

Everyone thought the band wouldn't last five minutes – five girls picked at random for a group were bound to start fighting, weren't they? But Girls Aloud bonded immediately. Although they were from different backgrounds and different places, there was a real girl-gang vibe about their friendship, which has grown stronger with time. They shared in common a dream, to make it as pop-stars, and this dream brought them together and made them one of the best girl groups in the world! Today the girls are so close that Cheryl can't imagine life without them.

"We've all grown into young women in the public eye," she says. "We are best friends. Looking back, I don't know how I lived without these girls."

The group was managed by Louis Walsh until 2005 when Hillary Shaw (who used to manage 80s girls band Bananarama) took over. That first Christmas, the group secured the Christmas Number 1, beating One True Voice, the boy band put together in *Popstars*. (One True Voice split up after only a couple of months.)

Cheryl couldn't believe Girls Aloud had made a hit record. "Four months ago I was sitting in a council house drinking tea and watching Oprah Winfrey all day," she says!

"We have to pinch ourselves. We're ordinary girls."

Cheryl on fame

The Passions of Girls Aloud

The Passions of Girls Aloud was a TV show, where each girl fulfilled a dream. Sarah learned to play polo in Argentina, Cheryl did some street-dancing in LA, Kimberley auditioned for a musical, and Nicola created a make-up range for pale skin. (Nadine was too busy to take part.)

A ROCKY START

Although the group had the Christmas hit, sales of their first album, *Sound of the Underground*, were a bit disappointing. Cheryl then hit the news when she allegedly hit a woman in a night-club. She was sentenced to community service, and started falling apart. She told the other girls that she was going to leave the band. "I was struggling mentally. I was having some terrible things said about me, feeling like the nation hated me," she says.

But she overcame it, and stayed with the girls.

"I feel like I'm a much stronger person for having gone through that experience," says Chez. "From every bad comes good and I learned a lot, especially about the media, and about myself."

Around the same time, the group weren't getting the support they felt they needed from manager Louis, either.

The girls knew they needed help. "We were a style disaster when we started out," says Cheryl. "We were anything but glamorous in un-co-ordinated clothes that didn't suit us. When we started touring, even though we'd been together for two years, we still had no idea what to do on stage. It's been a steep learning curve, but we're a lot wiser now." Although the girls were annoyed that Louis Walsh wasn't helping them as much as they needed, actually he did them a favour. By making them look after themselves and manage

Q: What's the worst video you've recorded?
A: "'Something Kinda Ooooh'. Because it's such a good song, it's disappointing the video was so bad," says Cheryl.

the band between them, they grew stronger and wiser than they would have done otherwise. "We learned a lot and we learned it fast," remembers Cheryl.

HITS

It was back in 2005 that the girls got serious about their style. The girls hired Christina Aguilera's stylist, Victoria Adcock, to put together a more mature look for them. Gone were the tracksuits and trainers, and the worries about their legs being too skinny – on went the heels, and now the girls love flashing their gorgeous pins! Cheryl in particular used to be a total tomboy, but today is regarded as one of the most fashionable women in the world!

It was also in 2005 that Girls Aloud released their third album, *Chemistry*, and started reaching the heights of popularity they enjoy today. Coldplay, the Arctic Monkeys, Oasis and the Pet Shop Boys all became fans. Today the group have sold millions of albums worldwide and won countless awards, including a Brit Award for Best Single, for 'The Promise'!

GIRLS TOGETHER
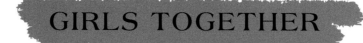

Although they spend a lot of time together, Girls Aloud get on like a house on fire. Touring is brilliant fun for them. "The best part of being in Girls Aloud is definitely being on tour," says Chez. "We absolutely love it!" The girls love the exciting stage routines, and doing things like being lowered on to the stage from the roof!

"One of the best times we have on tour is dancing to all the songs that we never release, all the album tracks that nobody's heard if they haven't bought the album," says Cheryl. "We like to bring them to life with choreography and having amazing dancers. It's always fun to have the boys on tour as well so you can have a laugh on the tour bus. Someone always gets stuck with having to make all the tea in the morning!"

There's always a lot of energy when the girls come off stage after a show – so much energy that things can get a little crazy on the tour bus, and they hardly get any sleep! But some of the girls are known for getting more crazy than the others – like party animal Sarah. Chez loves being on tour, because the posse have so much fun together – the girls and their crew. "We love our dancers," she says. "We always have lots of eccentric characters on the tour bus with us!"

Girls Aloud In Records

Studio Albums:
Sound of the Underground
What Will the Neighbours Say?
Chemistry
Tangled Up
Out of Control

Compilation/Remix albums:
The Sound of Girls Aloud:
 The Greatest Hits
Mixed Up
Girls A Live

UK Number One Singles:
Sound of the Underground
I'll Stand by You
Walk This Way
The Promise

"Girls Aloud have done very well,
it'd be great to work with them."

Gary Barlow, Take That

CHERYL'S GIRLS

Kimberley Walsh

Full name: Kimberley Jane Walsh

Nickname: Kimba

Date of Birth: 20th November 1981

Birthplace: Bradford, England

Star sign: Scorpio

Friends character she is most like: Monica Geller - because of her practical and organised nature

Thing she hates most: people farting!

Loves to: stay home and cook meals

Couldn't live without: mascara and lip gloss

Top make-up tip: "Practise makes perfect, so experiment with different make-up at home," she says

Beauty treat: she doesn't do anything out of the ordinary, and she doesn't buy into lotions and potions. But she'll

"Cheryl and Kimberley are the glue that holds the band together - and it's a very strong bond, too, which is why they work so well."

Louis Walsh, Girls Aloud former manager and X Factor judge

have a facial now and again, just for the pleasure of it.

Sarah Harding

Full name: Sarah Nicole Hardman (later changed to Harding)

Nickname: Saz

Date of Birth: 17th November 1981

Birthplace: Manchester, England

Star sign: Scorpio

Favourite food: Italian, Chinese, Mexican, Spanish and English!

Most embarrassing moment: falling over in a club in her best dress

Herself in three words: energetic, friendly and ambitious

Style secret: "When I was younger, I wouldn't go to school without putting on a full face of make-up about an inch thick. I was just so embarrassed if I had a spot. I'm not like that now, I'm much happier in my own skin," she says

Beauty routine: she loves the Estée Lauder facial range and Johnson's PH5.5 face wash.

"I could never, ever have envisaged them lasting so long … But they have survived, and it's down to no one else but themselves.

Louis Walsh, Girls Aloud former manager and X Factor *judge*

> "We're huge fans of Girls Aloud. They are all really talented. We were looking into taking the girls on a US tour this summer but the timings didn't work out. Next time we're going to make sure something does happen."
>
> *Kevin Jonas [Jonas Brothers]*

Nadine Coyle

Full name: Nadine Elizabeth Louise Coyle

Nickname: Nadz, Diney

Date of Birth: 15th June 1985

Birthplace: Derry, Ireland

Star sign: Gemini

Likes: singing, cooking and mucking around

Most embarrassing moment: falling over getting on a plane

First record bought: Kylie Minogue and Jason Donovan – 'Especially For You'

Describing herself: calm, confident, up for a laugh!

Big future: Nadine loves America. She has set up a beach bar in LA, called Nadine's Irish Mist. She also opened a restaurant in Florida and is refurbishing a Hollywood hotel.

Nicola Roberts

Full name: Nicola Maria Roberts

Date of Birth: 5th October 1985

Birthplace: Stamford, Lincolnshire, England

Star sign: Libra

What's in Nicola's bag on a night out: perfume, phone, credit card, house keys and make-up

First record bought: Spice Girls – 'Wannabee'

Favourite food: McDonald's

Trademark look: English rose – pale skin, red hair (Nicola has created a make-up range for pale girls, called Dainty Doll)

Style secret: ashamed of her pale skin, Nicola used to self-tan every night. But then she stopped faking it, and started to love being herself. "I use moisturiser, a bit of eye cream and lip balm and that's it," she says

Style future: Nicola was chosen to model for Vivienne Westwood because of her individual look.

"Me and Cheryl were like little chavs when we first moved to London. We were from rough places and we completely connected. We shared a flat and it was so cool, but honest to God it was a mess."
Nicola

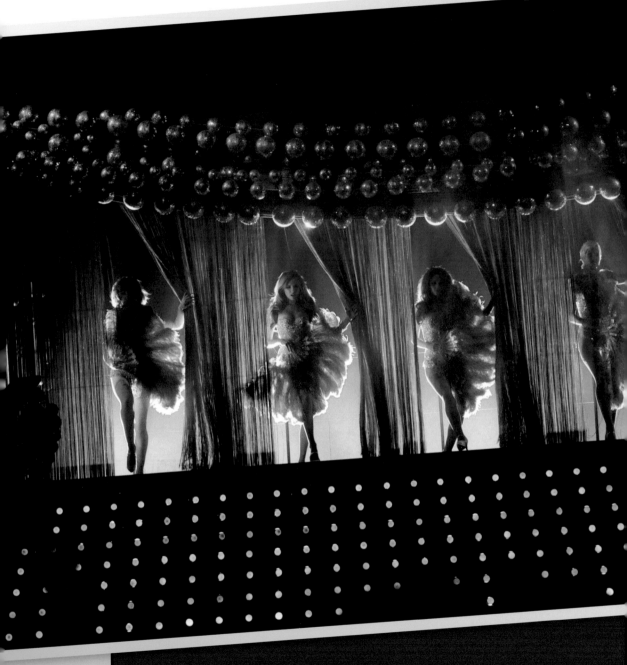

"Cheryl's so talented. If I only have a tiny bit of
the success Girls Aloud have had, I'll be happy."

Alex Burke on Girls Aloud

THE FUTURE FOR GIRLS ALOUD?

They've already released five hit studio albums and had a cameo in a film (*St Trinians*). At the moment the girls are all stars, shining brightly in their own right, so there have been many rumours about them splitting up – because of Cheryl's *X Factor* fame, or Nadine moving to LA. These rumours were all put to rest when the girls recently signed a new three-album deal with their label Polydor. To celebrate, Cheryl invited Nadine, Kimberley, Nicola and Sarah to her house for Christmas lunch. Hooray for our girls!

Imagine if Girls Aloud had all gone to school together!!

"We loved getting dressed up and going back to school for *St Trinian's*," says Cheryl. "I don't know what we would have all been like at school together. But we had so much fun on set just messing around. It REALLY was like being back at school."

"They're really cool and nice to work with. They're really chirpy and fun – a good bunch of girls."
James Morrison

X FACTOR
AND FAME

X FACTOR: BECOMING A JUDGE

When Sharon Osbourne announced she was leaving *X Factor*, the nation gasped. Who could they possibly get to replace Sharon, the show's mother hen? There were many rumours about who might step into her place, but there was one person Girls Aloud fans were cheering on: their Cheryl.

But Cheryl almost didn't make it as a judge – she refused Simon Cowell three times before finally agreeing! "I told him, not for all the tea in China," she says. "I didn't want to be in the position of judging someone. I didn't feel ready. I just knew, having been judged myself, how awful that felt. But he kept texting me and texting me and texting me and in the end I gave in. I couldn't help it.

"It's a massive honour to be following in the footsteps of Sharon Osbourne," she says. "The rest of the girls have said they're right behind me, which is really important for me as it will be weird to be on the other side of the fence this time."

As she'd been on the other side of the fence just five years before, no one understands what the contestants go through better than Cheryl. "No one else on the panel knows how it feels to be stood on that stage," she says. "They don't understand what it's like to be so young and have 12 million people watching you sing live every Saturday. What an immense amount of pressure."

X FACTOR: THE SERIES

The series was a rollercoaster ride of tears, laughter, tears, anger, more tears, joy – and then a bit more crying. As if we didn't know it already, Cheryl showed herself to have a heart of gold in her reactions to the contestants. When their performances were sad or moving, she cried – and she didn't care if millions of people across the country were watching her – because she knew we were all crying too!

"It looks like I'm always crying, but actually out of the thousands of auditions I've only been moved about four times," says Cheryl! "I've just always been quite a sensitive person. When you've got a grown man in front of you on the brink of tears, I don't know how you can't be moved."

"I think Cheryl is great. She's very knowledgeable about music. She has a go at Simon every minute, which he loves."

Dannii on Cheryl as a judge

It wasn't just the viewers who were won over by Cheryl. She won hundreds of celebrity supporters, including Girls Aloud's first manager – Louis Walsh. "I am so impressed with her on *X Factor* because she is real," says Louis. "Everyone identifies with her. She pretends she is tough on the outside, but on the inside she is very soft. She has a great head on her, a very good heart and she is still very ordinary beneath it all."

Cheryl also caught the eye of another judge: Simon Cowell. Louis Walsh noticed this too – "He definitely flirted with Dannii throughout the last series. But he seems to have moved on – he's flirting with Cheryl this season. He's definitely paying more attention to Cheryl now, not Dannii."

Many people predicted that *X Factor* would be nothing but a televised series of catfights between Dannii and Cheryl. But much to everyone's surprise – and some people's disappointment – the two girls got on just fine.

"Most of my friends are in their 30s, like Dannii, and she's in her prime," says Cheryl. "The horrible assumption that women working together must be jealous of each other is a stupid stereotype which is not true, because Girls Aloud wouldn't be here if it was."

"People just assume Cheryl and I won't get on, but I don't get it," says Dannii. "Why would I be upset that she's there?

Just because she's younger than me? That's kind of insulting to both of us."

There were a few bust-ups on the show between the judges – but not between Cheryl and Dannii, as people had thought. Instead, it was Cheryl and Simon that fell out (as well as Louis fighting with Dannii, and Louis and Simon squabbling all the way through the series). Cheryl got fired up at Simon, and raged at him: "You are doing my head in!"

In the same fiery episode, Cheryl also had words for ex-Girls Aloud manager Louis Walsh, saying to him that he knew nothing about girl groups.

"Girls Aloud didn't know anything when we started out. The beauty of *X Factor* is that the contestants have all watched it for years now. They know far more about what they're getting into than we ever did. I sit down and give them all the advice I can."

Cheryl on X Factor *contestants today*

CHERYL AND HER GIRLS

When it came to finding out who was going to mentor which group, Cheryl was keeping her fingers crossed to get the girls – which she did! The categories, which were handed out at random, left Simon with the boys, Dannii with the over-25s and Louis with the groups.

As the series went on, it became clear it wasn't just the viewers that loved Cheryl on the programme – her finalists also reported she was the best mentor. She helped them choose their songs, shared style tips and advised on what the girls should wear, and she even shared some deep secrets with them! One night she invited her hopefuls Alex Burke, Diana Vickers and Laura White out for dinner. Alex spills: "Everyone was very relaxed and we opened up about things in our lives and she opened up about things in hers. Cheryl has been through a lot in her life. She told us deep secrets – but we're not telling. She was very open with us. We even had a good old cry." All the girls were totally inspired by Cheryl, who would ring them every day to check if they were ok. What a sweetheart!

As the weeks went on, Cheryl's girls continued to win the hearts – and votes – of the viewers. There was nationwide outrage when Laura White was voted off in week five – viewers claimed a technical error hadn't counted their votes. That left just Alex and Diana from the Cheryl camp. The two girls were both going strong until the week nine semi-finals, when Diana Vickers was voted off. Controversy hit the headlines as Diana claimed that Cheryl had chosen the wrong songs for her. But Diana and Cheryl later made up.

"I love Cheryl!"

Pussycat Dolls star Melody Thornton

CHERYL AND ALEX

Cheryl had lots of words of wisdom for her remaining contestant, Alexandra Burke, telling her: "stay away from men!"

Cheryl was very clear on that front with Alex, who had recently broken up with her boyfriend before starting her *X Factor* journey. "Cheryl told me to keep away from men. She wants me to concentrate on music without any distractions," she says. "There will be no romance – I'm all about the music."

> "I've wanted this for so long. If it ended, I think I'd shrivel into a ball."

Cheryl on fame

Cheryl was annoyed with all the fighting and backstage egos on *X Factor*, and angry that the focus of the contest is all about which judge wins, rather than the contestant. "This isn't about me, Louis, whatever. No! None of the judges are going to win it. People don't vote for the judges. They vote for their favourite contestant . . . Alexandra will win it, not us. We're there to judge, to give advice, to build relationships with them. Of course, if one of my girls wins I'm going to go through the roof. But not because I'VE won. And I promise you I'm going to make damned sure one of my girls wins."

And it was a promise she kept!

THE FINAL

The week leading up to the *X Factor* final was tense for everyone – especially the ten million people watching on TV! Through the final week, in trying to prepare Alex the best she could, Cheryl often turned to Kimberley for advice on things like hair and make-up for her finalist. A dress was especially created by designer Suzanne Neville for Alex to wear in the final. Cheryl spent a lot of time watching over her final contestant, soothing Alex's nerves and getting her ready for her big day.

It was a really tough time for our Chez. The final was a really draining experience – but luckily, she had Girls Aloud bandmates Kimberley, Sarah and Nicola there supporting her. Hubby Ashley was away, preparing for a footy match.

> "I think Cheryl is a gorgeous girl, and Girls Aloud are really great – I like their music, Ruby [daughter] loves them."
>
> **Charlotte Church**

When Alex was announced as the winner, Chez burst into tears over and over again! Alex, totally buzzing about her win, couldn't have been happier. She beat off strong competition from Eoghan Quigg and boy group JLS, and sang a duet with Beyonce in the final. "Cheryl and I have united and become strong together, definitely. She is now my friend more than my mentor," says Alex. Cheryl has even given Alex a necklace with angel wings and a garnet stone, which Alex wears every day.

But the stress of the competition had obviously taken its toll on poor Cheryl, who looked exhausted. Many fans said they were concerned by how much weight she had lost. After the series was over, Cheryl took a well-deserved mini-break, a couple of days to relax and chill out.

CHERYL'S STYLE

These days, Cheryl always looks glam, whether she's on-stage, shopping, or heading out to party somewhere with the girls.

Although Cheryl confessed to being a tomboy when she was younger, today she's one of the most stylish women in the world – and has awards from the *Daily Mail* and *Tatler Magazine* (amongst others!) to prove it! But how does she pull these looks together, and what are her favourite outfits?

Cheryl Style Facts!

Favourite designers: Elie Saab, Dolce & Gabbana, Temperley, Hervé Léger, Chanel, Balmain, Azzedine Alaia

Most expensive item of clothing ever bought: a Hervé Léger dress

Cheapest item of clothing ever bought: a vest from Topshop, for £6.

"I love
Cheryl Cole."

Davina McCall

CLOTHES – DAYTIME

You could hardly call Cheryl casual – even when she's just
got off a 15-hour plane ride, our Chezza is always stylin'!
She LOVES wearing jeans, either super skinny to show
off her great pins, or high-waisted flares (which she loves
because they make her legs look longer). She's also been
spotted wearing threads from Justin Timberlake's jean
range, William Rast.

CLOTHES – EVENING WEAR

In case you hadn't noticed, Cheryl loves nothing more than glamming up. She loves: stunning wrap dresses with hot plunging necklines, 60s style shift dresses, and wow-factor minis, especially those with one shoulder strap. Hot stuff!

Cheryl also loves teaming belts with dresses to make the most of her figure (either wide belts or skinny ones, depending on the dress). Why not copy this style trick?

"Oh my God, Cheryl Cole! All of Girls Aloud are beautiful but Cheryl is just like, wow! British girls are great and I think their accent is very cute."

Joe Jonas [Jonas Brothers], on his crush on Cheryl

SHOES

Being teeny tiny like she is – 5 feet 3 inches – these days, Cheryl is rarely seen without her heels on. But one thing's for sure – whether they're towering punchy purple platforms or fabulous, zingy orange courts, they're always seriously hot! If you want to know a secret, how about this – Cheryl's got flat feet! "It's a Tweedy trait – they're like flippers! But my Terry de Havilland platforms (a gift from the designer) make them look quite elegant," she spills.

Get the look
MAKE-UP

The first thing you notice about Cheryl is those eyes – huge, dark brown, with thick eyelashes. She gets her look using an eyeshadow primer first – then layering her eyeshadow and eyeliner on top. Why not try using white eyeliner inside your lids for extra sparkle?

Our Chezza is always pout-perfect for the cameras too. She achieves her look using a long-lasting liner, and applying a slick of gloss for A-lister glamour! Chezza's also recently been snapped in shocking-pink lipstick, which is another hot trend for this year.

And let's not forget that tan. Cheryl is always looking her bronzed best, but if you're not lucky enough to live on the beach, try using a streakless fake tanner.

It's not all about expensive fashion secrets with Cheryl either – sometimes the best can be achieved by keeping it simple. "I've been using the same L'Oréal face wash for the past five years," she laughs. "I just make sure my face is clean, and that I'm cleansed and moisturised before I go to bed. Other than that, I don't have any secrets."

"I think Cheryl's beautiful. I have a bit of a weird girl crush on her."

Keisha Buchanan (Sugababes), on her little girl crush on Cheryl

Get the look
HAIR

"I love Cheryl.
She fancies me,
I'm telling you."

Amy Winehouse

For someone who claims to be happiest in a pair of trackies, Cheryl always has perfect hair! To keep your tresses in perfect condition like Cheryl, make sure you pamper your hair weekly with a special intensive conditioner.
When it comes to styling, make sure you do big hair, just like Cheryl does! To get that look, spray a volume enhancing product on to the roots of your towel-dried hair. For added lift, why not get a friend to help you back-comb it, for that sassy 60s vibe that Cheryl does so well!

CHERYL AND HER INSECURITIES

If you've ever woken up, looked in the mirror and thought you looked totally blah, don't worry – it happens to everyone, including our gorgeous Cheryl! As someone who's never liked her legs, Cheryl understands what it feels like to look in the mirror and be disappointed by what you see. She hopes that people will feel better knowing that about her.

"I don't like my legs. I haven't got much of them for a start. It's just the thing that I don't like so if I was dressing myself I'd probably cover them up," she says.

And that's not all. Just like you and me, Cheryl has days when she just can't get her outfit right either. "There will be times when I've got changed three or more times before I leave the house," she says. "Could be hormones, bad hair day, feel fat or spotty. I have it all."

Cheryl has insecurities about a lot of things, and relates to women who have issues with their bodies. "But when I look in the mirror every morning, I have to tell you, I never go 'yuck'," she adds. "I may not think I'm the sexiest person alive, but what I do see is a successful woman who is doing what she loves."

"She's beautiful, not just to look at but as a person. *X Factor* is great because people get to see her cry, see her real personality."

Ashley Cole

She says: "If somebody sees a bit of cellulite on my legs that's been circled in a magazine and it makes them feel comfortable then I'm happy that I've made that one person at home go, 'Cheryl's got cellulite, it's fine.' I do it myself. I flick through magazines and see Kate Moss has got cellulite and it makes me feel happier about myself. You can't help it."

Cheryl thinks the media has a lot to do with the way women feel about their bodies today, and says there's too much pressure on women about their size these days: "Girls are constantly being told they're either too fat or too thin, which is irresponsible." Cheryl – who has had her weight criticised by the media repeatedly – goes on to say: "If you're fat they say you're too fat, if you're looking thin, they say you're too thin and if you don't have any make-up on they say you're ugly. I want to eat healthily, I don't want to be clogging my arteries up with crap or eating McDonald's every day, but that's got nothing to do with what the media has to say."

49

STRUGGLES WITH HER WEIGHT

Cheryl has always had a small frame, which gets noticeably smaller when the Geordie celeb is stressed out. After a bad break-up when she was a teenager, Cheryl lost so much weight her friends and family were seriously worried about her.

Her nearest and dearest voiced concern again after the *X Factor* final. And they weren't the only ones – after seeing the final on TV, Cheryl herself couldn't believe how much weight she had lost, and thought she looked terrible and unhealthy. 2008 was a stressful year for her – she had to deal with marital problems with hubby Ashley, and *X Factor* put the pressure on, too. Her weight just plummeted. So, in preparation for climbing Mount Kilimanjaro to raise money for Comic Relief, Cheryl went on a New Year's diet – to put on some pounds!

"Cheryl is the most beautiful woman in the world. I could look at her for hours."

Rebecca Loos

Cheryl's shopping secrets

Cheryl buys most of her clothes from Net-a-Porter.com instead of going round the shops, and she gets silk wraps done by a girl she has known for ages who always comes to her home, as she's a bit mistrustful of beauticians and hairdressers these days.

51

ROMANCE
& RUMOURS

It's no secret that Cheryl is married to celebrity footballer Ashley Cole. But what about her romantic past? Well, she may live the fairytale life of a popstar, but just like you and me, Cheryl's also had her share of heartbreaks.

TEENAGE LOVE

After a painful break-up when she was a teenager, Cheryl admits to losing so much weight that she looked like she was almost dead. "For two years I was in a really destructive relationship," she says. "I'd been clinically depressed and dangerously underweight. I was having terrible panic attacks and suffered from anxiety, and as a result my appetite went. Any food used to make my stomach churn. I was 5st 11lb at my worst point, like a walking corpse."

But poor Cheryl picked herself up, dusted herself off, and went on to compete in *Popstars: The Rivals*, where she met fellow contestant Jacob Thompson. The pair took an instant liking to each other, but sadly, their romance didn't last. When Cheryl was picked for Girls Aloud, she made the decision to concentrate on her career – and that meant no boys. Poor Jacob – who went back to his old job as a carpet fitter - was kicked to the kerb.

CHERYL AND ASHLEY

When Cheryl first met future hubby Ashley Cole, they were both living in the same apartment block. Cheryl wasn't looking for a relationship when they met, and she wasn't fussed about him at first. "I saw him playing tennis and he'd look at me like he fancied me, you know! I'd tut and look away. One day he asked for my number and I said no in front of all his friends!" she says.

But a couple of weeks later she saw Ashley in a magazine, looking cute, and changed her mind about him.

Cheryl's tips on getting the guy you want!

"Play hard to get. Don't call him, don't text him, and he'll come running to you. It works every time," she says.

THEIR FIRST DATE

Ashley was so nervous about his first date with Cheryl that he took a friend with him! While that's obviously cute factor ten, it killed the mood a bit for Chezza. "It was a bit uncomfortable for me," she says.

But eventually Ashley's friend left, and he and Cheryl had a couple of glasses of wine, and that was it. According to Cheryl, they just clicked.

"Pretty soon after we met I knew something was different and I knew I had never felt that before," she gushes.

"Girls Aloud wouldn't break up if I had a baby, but it would change the dynamics. We have been working non-stop and there will come a time when you have to prioritise things, but I'm just focused on what I'm doing with the girls right now."

Cheryl on having babies

AN UNEXPECTED PROPOSAL

Cheryl and Ashley had only been dating for eight months when Ashley popped the question! The couple were on a private holiday in Dubai at the time. The pair took a romantic camel ride together – then afterwards, Ashley dropped to one knee and proposed with a £50,000 diamond ring! Not a bad way to get engaged. Cheryl was over the moon, and said it was fantastic. She had no idea he was going to propose – he made her dreams come true!

Q: Who in the whole world would Simon Cowell most like to kiss?

A: Guess what – it's our Cheryl! He confessed: "I'm going to get into so much trouble after this. I want a disclaimer first of all that I'm going to say this person as if they weren't married . . . so I am going to say Cheryl Cole." He went on to say, "Who wouldn't?"!

THE WEDDING

Cheryl and Ashley got married in July 2006. Cheryl did everything for the wedding. She picked the location, which was to be Highclere Castle, Hampshire, until she discovered that was where Jordan and Peter were getting married, so she changed it to Wrotham Park, Hertfordshire. Cheryl also chose the menu (prawn cocktail followed by steak and chips, because both her and Ashley come from working class backgrounds and she didn't want posh food!), and she also picked their outfits, both designed by Roberto Cavalli.

About her wedding day, Cheryl says:

"It was honestly the happiest moment of my life. He's everything I ever wanted in a relationship."

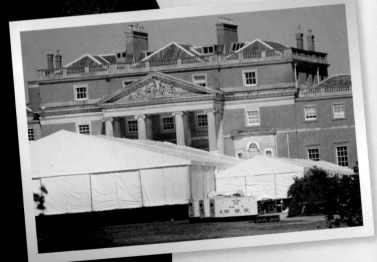

"Cheryl is the new Queen WAG, not Posh. And she's obviously jealous. When Cheryl's husband allegedly cheated on her, she was honest about everything to her fans."

Nicola McLean

TROUBLES

But alas, the fairytale wasn't to last. The couple have suffered a rocky time, as there were upsetting kiss-and-tell stories in the newspapers that threatened to ruin their relationship.

Poor Cheryl was totally devastated by it all. Her weight plunged to a terrifying six stone, and she hid away in her flat for two weeks, and tried to forget about everything by putting everything into Girls Aloud. But she was so exhausted that the group's manager paid for her to fly out to a Thai island with other Girls Aloud members Nicola and Kimberley, to relax and try to get over it.

After her Thai retreat, Cheryl threw herself back into her work with Girls Aloud, and got some well-needed loving from her faithful pooch, Buster!

GETTING BACK TOGETHER

After months of pain, Cheryl – who has a heart of gold – couldn't ignore her emotions. Cheryl's also a very traditional girl at heart, and took the marriage vows – for better or worse – very seriously. She was still in love with Ashley, and decided to give it another chance.

"People make mistakes, stuff happens," she says. "Ashley's a free spirit. I'm not his keeper. I believe in letting people live their lives and be free, so Ashley can have time with his friends when he wants, he can go out when he wants."

The whole experience must have been really upsetting for Cheryl. "I can't hurt any more than I've been hurt, I can't cry any more than I've cried," she says. "I've been to the highest of highs and lowest of lows, so one day I'm going to find my middle ground and be happy."

Just as things had begun to look brighter for the couple, Cheryl and Ashley were back in the headlines again. While Cheryl was climbing Mount Kilimanjaro to raise money for Comic Relief, Ashley was out partying and got arrested. The timing couldn't have been worse and being front page news again must have been really difficult for them both. But once again, they seem to be working things out and Cheryl's back to her gorgeous smiley self! And who knows what 2010 will bring to Cheryl and Ashley's marriage, perhaps the patter of tiny feet?

"I wouldn't wish what Cheryl's been through on anybody. It must just be awful."

Dannii Minogue

59

THE FUTURE

After achieving so much at such a young age, what could there possibly be left for Cheryl to do? She's already earned an estimated £5 million from Girls Aloud, various advertising deals and being an *X Factor* judge – but money has never meant much to our Cheryl. She's far too grounded for that!

She's definitely got some tricks up her sleeve though. As well as future series of *X Factor*, she's keen to do more solo work, following up her appearance on the song 'Heartbreaker' with will.i.am from the Black Eyed Peas (who is a big Cheryl fan). She's has also been offered a deal to release her own range of chick-lit novels – so perhaps this time next year you might be reading some Chezza-fiction!

One thing's for certain – the bubbly brunette will have her hands full. Cheryl has her sights set on conquering America! But with support from American celebs

"I love Cheryl! I'm obsessed with her. I just think she's amazing!"

Will Young

like Paris Hilton and Melody Thornton of the Pussycat Dolls, surely she's got that in the bag?

Stay tuned for the next chapter in Cheryl's life. It promises to be action-packed!

61

PICTURE CREDITS

Getty: 4, 5, 7 (left), 11, 15, 20 (left), 23 (bottom), 25, 27, 29, 30, 31, 45 (top & bottom), 46, 48, 50, 53, 55 (bottom), 56 (left), 60

Rex: 2, 3, 7 (right), 14, 16, 17, 18, 19 (bottom), 21, 32, 34, 35, 36, 37, 38, 39, 40, 41, 43 (right), 47 (right), 56 (right), 59, 61

PA Photos: 6, 8, 9, 10, 12, 13, 19 (top), 20 (right), 22, 24, 26, 28, 42, 43 (left & centre), 44, 45 (middle), 47 (left), 51, 52, 54, 55 (top), 57, 58

Catwalking: 49

ACKNOWLEDGEMENTS

Posy Edwards would like to thank Helia Phoenix, Amanda Harris, Helen Ewing, Jane Sturrock, Frank Brinkley, Briony Hartley and Rich Carr.

First published in hardback in Great Britain in 2009 by Orion Books an imprint of the Orion Publishing Group Ltd
Orion House, 5 Upper St Martin's Lane, London WC2H 9EA
An Hachette Livre UK Company

1 3 5 7 9 10 8 6 4 2

A CIP catalogue record for this book is available from the British Library.

ISBN: 978 1 4091 1362 1

Designed by Goldust Design
Printed in Spain by Cayfosa

The Orion Publishing Group's policy is to use papers that are natural, renewable and recyclable and made from wood grown in sustainable forests. The logging and manufacturing processes are expected to conform to the environmental regulations of the country of origin.

Every effort has been made to fulfil requirements with regard to reproducing copyright material. The author and publisher will be glad to rectify any omissions at the earliest opportunity.